PRESIDENT GARFIELD'S KILLER AND THE AMERICA HE LEFT BEHIND

THE ASSASSIN, THE CRIME, THE HAPLESS DOCTORS, AND A PRESIDENT'S SLOW, GRIM DEATH

COMPASS POINT BOOKS
a capstone imprint

With love to my dad and hero, Jesse Tougas. –JT

Assassins' America is published by Compass Point Books, a Capstone imprint
1710 Roe Crest Drive, North Mankato, Minnesota 56003
www.mycapstone.com

Library of Congress Cataloging-in-Publication Data
Names: Tougas, Joe, author.
Title: President Garfield's killer and the America he left behind : the assassin, the crime, the hapless doctors, and a president's slow, grim death / by Joe Tougas.
Description: North Mankato, Minnesota : Compass Point Books, 2018. | Series: Assassins' America | Audience: Ages 9-15.
Identifiers: LCCN 2017042670 (print) | LCCN 2017043545 (ebook) | ISBN 9780756557232 (eBook pdf) | ISBN 9780756557157 (hardcover) | ISBN 9780756557195 (pbk.)
Subjects: LCSH: Garfield, James A. (James Abram), 1831-1881—Assassination—Juvenile literature. | Garfield, James A. (James Abram), 1831-1881—Death and burial—Juvenile literature. | Guiteau, Charles J. (Charles Julius), 1841-1882—Juvenile literature.
Classification: LCC E687.9 (ebook) | LCC E687.9 .T68 2018 (print) | DDC 973.8/4092—dc23
LC record available at https://lccn.loc.gov/2017042670

Editorial Credits
Nick Healy, editor; Mackenzie Lopez and Kay Fraser, designers; Svetlana Zhurkin, media researcher; Tori Abraham, production specialist

Printed and bound in the United States of America.
010749S18

TABLE OF CONTENTS

CHAPTER 1
AN UNLIKELY PRESIDENT

Imagine you've been assigned to write a long research paper on any U.S. president. It's due soon. Like tomorrow. And for the fun of it, let's also say you haven't done a thing yet. Suddenly, you need to think and work fast, and the first move is choosing your subject.

George Washington? Abraham Lincoln? Thomas Jefferson? Extraordinary leaders, all of them. They lived amazing lives in momentous times, achieving a greatness that forever shaped the United States. Such greatness will also keep you up all night researching and writing.

No, you need to pick a president who didn't change our world all that much, somebody to whom history books devote small, handy chapters. This may lead you to President James Garfield, who was in office for only a few short months before he was shot.

You may already see your report taking shape: elected, shot, died, and done. Simple, right? Maybe. But be warned: You may accidentally find yourself drawn in when you learn about James Garfield. And you may find yourself sorry that he wasn't president for longer, because Garfield might have been a great president — another one of those people remembered for shaping his country.

Garfield was an early believer in civil rights, and with former slaves being brutalized by whites in the South, civil rights needed believers, especially at the presidential level. He also pledged to take a firm stand against government officials who took part in crooked, unfair practices that rewarded favors instead of honest work for the American people. He gave hope to working families across the country because he knew what it was like to grow up poor and how miserable it could be.

Garfield seemed ready to fight for the kind of changes that were overdue in the United States. The Civil War had ended about 15 years earlier, but the country was not making good on its promises of freedom and equality for all. Former slaves found their freedoms limited in new ways. Racial prejudice prevailed in many places and ways. Because he was gunned down four months after taking office, Garfield was unable to finish — or even really begin — what he wanted to accomplish.

Born in Ohio, Garfield was the kind of person others talk about when they mention America as a land of opportunity, a country where people can succeed no matter where they begin. As a boy, Garfield's life was marred by sadness and extreme poverty. As a man, he was a leader who, in a desire to help his fellow Americans, rose to the office of president of the United States.

As a boy James Garfield worked as a mule rider towing canal boats.

Garfield's father moved to Ohio from New York in the early 1800s, first helping build the Ohio and Erie Canal, then making a go as a farmer. He married Eliza Ballou, and the couple farmed in the Ohio countryside. Sadly, James, born November 19, 1831, never knew his father, who died when the future president was 1 year old.

Following her husband's death, Eliza Garfield worked hard to not only put food on the table but to keep her four kids at home. In those days poverty often tore families apart, and the Garfields were indeed poor. James didn't get a pair of shoes until he was 4 years old. The home his family shared was a one-room log cabin with three small windows, the panes of which were oiled paper.

James Garfield at age 14

In such situations, the people often sent their children away to better-off homes with hope of giving them a comfortable life. Although Eliza was encouraged to do this, she kept her children. She tried to make the best of their poor conditions. She knew that education held James' key to escaping a future of poverty, but his interests were more in the working life, like his father.

Eager to work on the water, James at age 16 took work as a canal man on the Erie and Ohio Canal. His time in that job proved to be dangerous. Unable to swim, he nearly drowned after falling off the boat one evening, and shortly afterward, he contracted malaria. The disease, which is caused by a parasite infecting the blood, killed many of its victims. With her son at risk of an early death, James' mother offered him the grand total of $17 in hopes he would use it to go back to school.

Believing that his life was spared for a reason, James agreed to start attending school. From local schools he went to northern Ohio, where he enrolled in a small prep school called Western Reserve Eclectic Institute. He earned his tuition by working as a janitor for the school. James took to his subjects with great passion and fascination.

His school work was so successful that the school promoted him from janitor to professor. While in his second year of studies,

Mollie, Harry, James, Irving, and Abe Garfield (from left) were five of James and Lucretia Garfield's seven children.

James also began teaching classes including literature, math, and ancient languages.

In 1854 he was accepted to Williams College in Williamstown, Massachusetts, opening the world to him even further. He graduated with honors and returned to Ohio to teach at the Western Reserve Eclectic Institute. He became the school's president at age 26.

In 1858 Garfield married a former student of his from Western Reserve Eclectic Institute, Lucretia Rudolph. After Lucretia graduated, she and Garfield had exchanged letters, growing quite fond of each other. They would go on to have two daughters and five sons.

Garfield entered the world of politics in 1859 when a state senator died. Garfield was encouraged to run in an upcoming election, and he did so successfully. The Civil War soon interrupted his political career. He had hardly settled into office when the war broke out.

Eager to join the Union Army, he was made lieutenant colonel and showed himself to be a smart military thinker and strategist. In the Battle of Middle Creek, he fooled the Confederates into thinking his regiment was larger than it was. In attacking the much larger Confederate regiment from three sides, the appearance was enough to send the Confederates retreating and out of Kentucky. The battle made him famous. He was made a general, and ten months later in 1862, he was elected to the U.S. Congress.

In Congress, Garfield believed part of his role was to help the people like those he lived with as child, studied with as a student, and fought with as a soldier. He helped create jobs in the areas of

Garfield rose to the rank of major general during the Civil War.

westward expansion — the development of roads, businesses, and communities in western states. He was particularly passionate about civil rights for African Americans. To that end, he introduced a measure that allowed black people to walk freely in Washington, D.C., without a pass. Today it may boggle the mind to think such a law would be necessary. In Garfield's time, racial prejudice had powerful friends in politics. Garfield and others fought for small victories for fairness and equality.

As a congressman, Garfield gave an acclaimed speech in support of allowing African Americans the right to vote when the war ended. He proved to be a strong ally of President Abraham Lincoln. Garfield won reelection overwhelmingly in 1864.

Sixteen years later, with the Civil War long over, President Lincoln's assassination remained a wound the nation hadn't healed. In 1880 the Republicans sent delegates to Chicago to choose their next nominee for president. By then Lincoln's party was divided into two groups, known as the Stalwarts and the Half-Breeds. The Stalwart Republicans — led by Senator Roscoe Conkling of New York, were those who enjoyed and benefitted from the spoils system. Under the spoils system, politicians gave powerful jobs as rewards to friends for their votes, money, or other forms of loyalty.

Conkling owed his wealth and power to the spoils system. He oversaw The New York Customs House, which handled most of the money that came in from taxing imports. He gave jobs — often with very good pay — to his political friends, and he steered government policy to reward the people and business that supported him. With such power, Conkling could control many politicians. Those who opposed his wishes could find themselves without a job. Conkling wanted to make sure the spoils system remained in place.

★ ★ ★

The Republican Party's convention in 1880 took place in Chicago, and it was a long, complicated, and testy affair. The party had a sitting president in the White House, but Rutherford B. Hayes had decided not to seek a second term. At the convention, Conkling and the Stalwarts aimed to nominate Ulysses S. Grant. The heroic general from the Civil War had already served two terms as president, from 1869 to 1877. The Stalwarts wanted to send him back for a third term, something no president had ever done.

The Half-Breed group, however, aimed to make James G. Blaine the party's candidate. Blaine was a senator from Maine, and he had previously served in the U.S. House of Representatives. He was also engaged in a political feud with Conkling and his allies. A third candidate, John Sherman of Ohio, also vied for delegates at the convention. Sherman was a former senator from Garfield's home state of Ohio, and Sherman was Secretary of the Treasury under Hayes. Sherman made a difficult candidate, though. His personality was so calm and reserved that he'd been nicknamed the Ohio Icicle.

As a delegate in Chicago, Conkling gave a speech to support Ulysses S. Grant, considered the favorite to be nominated as the Republican choice for president. On the first ballot, Grant got 304 votes, while Blaine had 285 and Sherman a mere 93. To get the nomination, a candidate would need 379 votes. Speeches were made, and more votes were taken. Through more than 30 ballots, no man reached the total required to be the party's nominee.

Garfield was well known as a good senator, a gifted writer, and a dynamic speaker. At the convention, his speech given in support of fellow Ohioan John Sherman proved this. The speech drew thunderous applause, and Garfield himself drew attention from many of the delegates.

Eventually his name was submitted at the convention as a possible Republican candidate for the presidency. He wasn't interested in the job and likely didn't think his name would rise in the convention voting. But he was wrong. Party delegates voted again and again. Grant never mustered enough support to claim the nomination. Two days and more voting later, the nomination went to the one man who wanted it least: James Garfield.

He was less than thrilled. Having seen good men run ragged in their desire to be president, Garfield had no personal interest in the job. But he also believed he could make a difference — perhaps where previous presidents could not. He believed this was his purpose. Shortly after receiving and accepting the nomination, he told a well-wisher, "I am very sorry that this has become necessary."

As the nominee, he faced off against Democrat Winfield Scott Hancock, a Civil War hero who had no experience in public office. The election was too close to call on election day itself, and Garfield went to bed before the votes were tallied. He woke up to the news that he was elected president. Garfield began making plans to move with his family, including his mother (a very proud Eliza Garfield) to Washington, D.C.

Mere months later in that city he would be shot at a train station. He would die not only from the wound, but from the shoddy medical care he received.

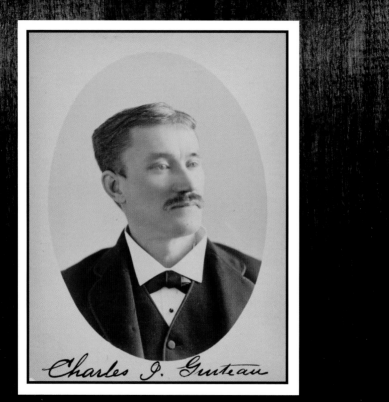

Charles J. Guiteau

CHAPTER 2
GARFIELD'S KILLER

Both James Garfield and his killer, Charles Guiteau, believed they were put on Earth to do something special. Garfield thought his purpose was to make people's lives better. And after a life that included being a teacher and war hero, becoming president was his biggest opportunity yet to do just that. At that same time, Guiteau would begin telling people he believed that he was put on Earth to kill President Garfield.

Looking at the lives of these two men, opposite tales emerge. With each chance Garfield took and with each new adventure — whether attending college, leading soldiers, or running for political office — he was a winner. Charles Guiteau, just as ambitious, seemed to meet failure at every turn. As Garfield's successes mounted, the life of Charles Guiteau seemed to collapse. He finally snapped, sending him toward one violent act that resulted in Garfield's death and, eventually, in Guiteau's own death.

It's a tragic story, the life of Charles Guiteau. Up until his murderous act, you could almost feel sorry for him. In fact, in today's world, he would be likely recognized as having serious mental illness and needing treatment and therapy. And although there were homes and treatments for obviously insane people, as he might have been called in his day, he never received any such help.

Guiteau's youth began on an Illinois farm where, after losing his mother when he was 7, he was raised by his father, Luther Guiteau. (Their last name is pronounced GEH-TOE.) Luther was a religious zealot who thought he was so close to God he would live forever. He also believed the goal of humans was to be perfect. On that point, his son disappointed him. For instance, Charles was physically weak and had a hard time talking. Throughout his childhood, Charles' father would burst into fits of rage — mocking, belittling, and beating his son.

Guiteau wanted so badly to please his father that he took on the same kind of religious beliefs as he grew older. At age 18 he joined a religious group in upstate New York led by his father's religious instructor, John Humphrey Noyes.

Noyes led a small religious community named Oneida. It had about 300 members. These members were allowed, and even encouraged, to have several romantic partners. Even with those kinds of rules, Guiteau had trouble finding anybody interested in him. This was likely because he insisted he was above everybody, that he was chosen by God to be there and that he should be treated better than others. He was, by all accounts, incredibly annoying. As a result, he found himself alone and rejected more than a few times. His nickname among the women of Oneida was "Charles Gitout" (as in "Get OUT!")

After living there six years, Guiteau left in 1865 and attempted to start a religious newspaper. That proved to be more work than he expected, and he gave up after four months, returning for another year to Oneida.

Guiteau's failures were epic in work and in love. After Oneida, in 1869, he married a young librarian named Annie Bunn, whose later descriptions of her four years with him were terrifying. He was violent with her, even locking her in a closet at times. She felt he was "possessed of an evil spirit" and divorced him.

After his failure as a newsman, Guiteau took on work as a lawyer. If you were in any sort of trouble with the law, you did not want Charles Guiteau as your lawyer. Back then, being a lawyer didn't require someone to go to law school and pass a state exam. Guiteau clearly needed a bit of legal education. His work as a lawyer in New York and Chicago quickly became famous for how weird he was in court and how he seemed more interested in preaching religion than defending a client.

During Guiteau's 14 years working as a lawyer, he persistently tried to convince wealthy Chicago citizens to help him buy one of the city's most successful newspapers. He promised to give them great coverage should they run for political office. But he couldn't find a wealthy backer. Perhaps they saw through Guiteau's soaring ego or noted his unsteady personality, or both. Nobody, it seemed, was interested in going into business with him.

Uninterested in law and out of luck when it came to buying a newspaper, he tried making money by returning to religion.

Guiteau traveled the country as a preacher. He would arrive in cities, advertise his upcoming appearances, and end up preaching to small groups. He found little success in this new pursuit. Many listeners heckled him while he spoke or simply walked away.

As he moved through life and its many disappointments, Guiteau remained certain he was somehow meant for a larger purpose. This is likely how he convinced himself that it was OK to cheat landlords — that he was somehow above the law. He wasn't above the law, of course, but he was often out of money. He had a system of staying in fine boarding houses and sneaking out on his last day without paying. Occasionally the law caught up with him. Guiteau spent at least some time in jail for failure to pay in 1874.

As time went on and he needed money, Guiteau began begging family members for loans. His sister was helpful at first, offering not only money but a place to live with her family in Wisconsin. But Guiteau soon enough had his sister fearing for her life. Once he stood near her and raised the ax he had been using to cut wood. She tried to have her brother put into a mental hospital, but he left Wisconsin before she had the chance.

Guiteau roamed from town to town and from boarding house to boarding house.

His further attempts to make money included suing people and organizations including the commune where he lived for years. Claiming he was owed money for the work he did at Oneida, Guiteau threatened to sue Reverend Noyes. But when Guiteau's own lawyer realized Guiteau's reputation for doing very little work, he walked away from the case.

It was Noyes who told Guiteau's father the sad truth: Charles

Roscoe Conkling of New York was a powerful figure in the Republican Party.

Guiteau was clearly insane. Charles' father and brother were also convinced he should be put away and regretted they did not have the money to put him in an asylum.

In 1880, after dodging landlords and others to whom he owed money, Charles Guiteau drifted into Boston. There he became fascinated with politics. He read with great interest about Roscoe Conkling, a rich and powerful senator from New York. It was well known that Conkling could make others rich if they were loyal to him and the Stalwarts. The spoils system, or "machine" politics, was thriving in Washington, D.C.

This, Guiteau thought, would be his way into the fame that he deserved. He quickly decided he would work for the Republican Party and be, like Conkling, a Stalwart.

He took a great interest in the upcoming presidential election and made sure he got himself into as many campaign meetings and rallies as possible. He desperately hoped to make a name for himself among the powerful leaders of the Republican party, believing he would eventually be given an important job with the government.

Three days after Garfield was selected as the Republican candidate for president, Guiteau went to New York to campaign on his behalf and hand out copies of a speech he had written in Boston praising Garfield. He frequently approached Chester Arthur, offering him copies of the speech. A powerful Republican, Arthur at one point agreed to let Guiteau deliver the speech at a small gathering in New York. In this, his only delivery of the speech, Guiteau choked — talking for only a few minutes and claiming it was too hot.

A magazine caricature of Guiteau after his arrest

Guiteau nonetheless carried copies of the speech, handing them out to Republican Party leaders he met. He insisted the speech helped Garfield win the presidential election of 1880. Guiteau, in fact, believed the new president would be so grateful for Guiteau's speech and help with the campaign that he would give Guiteau exactly the job he wanted. He wished to be an American ambassador — a consul — to Paris, France.

That was, after all, how the political machine worked. The problem was, Garfield intended to stop the spoils system. He wanted to give jobs to people who could perform them well, not to those who did him favors.

With Garfield in the White House, Guiteau moved to Washington, D.C., convinced the new president would appoint him to the job he sought. But Guiteau would have to wait a while. A LOT of people wanted jobs.

Garfield's first months as president were spent making appointments to more than 800 government jobs. Guiteau went to the White House at least 15 times, waiting to speak with the new president or his secretary of state, James Blaine, to discuss the Paris job. If he was told to wait or treated in a way he disliked, Guiteau would explain his importance. He would announce that his speech had won the election for Garfield.

In this time, as in so many others, Guiteau's attempts to impress important people simply backfired. One senator later said he would not have recommended this strange man for any job. "I treated him as kindly and as politely as I could," the senator said, "but I was very desirous of getting rid of him."

Guiteau eventually was granted a brief meeting with President Garfield. One on one with the president, Guiteau explained his support, offering the president a copy of his published speech. On the cover, Guiteau had written "Paris Consulship" and his name.

Guiteau left the meeting confident he'd get the job. He continued visiting the White House, walking among visitors, staff, and others. He was drawing attention to himself but not in the way he'd hoped. At one point he attended a public function — a reception at the presidential mansion — and walked up to the first lady, introduced himself, and handed her his business card.

After politely dealing with dozens of encounters with Guiteau at the State Department, Secretary of State Blaine finally told him the truth. He said Guiteau had "no prospect whatsoever" of receiving the Paris job from the president.

For the next several months, Guiteau remained in Washington, D.C. He was friendless, broke, and continually writing to the president with suggestions, including that he get rid of Blaine. By this time, Guiteau had been banned from the White House over his odd behavior, and his continued letters were placed in what was basically an "ignore" folder.

Guiteau would say, during his trial and imprisonment, that it was two months after meeting with Garfield that he first heard an instruction from God. According to Guiteau, the voice of God told him Garfield needed to be "removed" from office and Guiteau needed to make it happen with a gun.

Garfield was presented to voters as the candidate for honesty in government.

CHAPTER 3
A POLITICAL MESS

In seeking to win the presidency of 1880, James Garfield had two major issues on his mind. One was a result of his own upbringing: to take care of the working people in the country, especially those who until recently had been enslaved. He was also determined to undo what he saw taking place throughout his career in Congress: a political system that allowed many men to become rich and powerful for the wrong reasons.

Neither of these ideas was going to go over well with everyone in his own party. But Garfield was a man of honor and vision, and his time was a challenging one for anyone who wanted to change a system that was heading in the wrong direction.

That system of dishing out good jobs or other favors to loyal "friends" was called the spoils system. The name came from the saying "to the victor go the spoils," meaning that the winner of a war gets to enjoy all the riches and comforts that used to belong to the enemy — money, land, possessions, etc.

When political candidates won office in the early and mid-1800s, they usually made sure to reward the loyal party members who helped them get elected.

In the years that Garfield was a U.S. senator, he saw how these spoils meant giving good jobs to people who didn't deserve them and knew very little about the work involved. The spoils system wasn't necessarily illegal. Presidents were given the power to appoint whomever they pleased. But too often jobs went to friends and supporters, not qualified people who would help the country thrive.

At that time, money was flowing into the U.S. economy in levels never seen before. Outside of government, the growth of factories and the Industrial Revolution brought rapid change to the United States. It was hard to keep cities clean, and it was hard to keep rich men and government leaders honest.

And as industry grew and factories rose, the owners of those industries found themselves in a world of riches that few could imagine. In desperate need of jobs, poor people found opportunities to work. The rush to these factories resulted in dramatic growth in the number of Americans living in cities.

Factories were running hard while the workers in them were forced to work long days (10- or 12-hour days were typical) in often unsafe and unhealthy conditions. This caused little concern from the factory owners, who kept the bulk of the money to themselves and made sure they contributed to their government officials to ensure favors in the future. The workers who were putting in such long hours? They had no power to complain, and they would lose their jobs if they did.

In the late 1800s industrial growth changed the lives of urban workers, such as the many people who worked in this soap factory in New York City.

These were the people Garfield thought of when he entered government and when he fought against unfair practices. His own experience with poverty had inspired him to run for office in the first place. He'd hoped to make a difference for the working people of America. Those were people who were not rich and did not have powerful friends handing out money and favors. In other words, most Americans.

Garfield knew full well what hard-working people in America had to put up with just to survive. He need only remember his mother's hard work raising his family to understand the difficulty so many families faced. Because of this, he took his role as a senator quite differently from those who saw the U.S. Congress as a place to swing deals and reward friends. He'd entered political office with hopes of helping make the country a good place for everyone, no matter their wealth.

It bothered him that the country, which held such promise and had given him so much opportunity, was being soured by politicians who were creating laws to serve the wealthy class and its friends. It was as though you were either in or out of the club. Most people were out, and the club took care if its own.

By the time Garfield's name was mentioned in the presidential contest, the Republican Party had become divided over the spoils system. Those Republicans calling themselves Stalwarts wanted not only to keep the spoils system in place; they were also against making peace with the Southern states in the long aftermath of the Civil War. The spoils system benefitted the Stalwarts, and it benefitted companies that helped them financially. Regular Americans worked hard for very little while lawmakers and their rich friends kept the money at the top.

The Stalwarts presented an incredibly strong force in the party. In fact, when President Rutherford B. Hayes criticized the spoils system, Stalwarts made work miserable and difficult for him. Hayes decided he would refuse to accept nomination for a second term, claiming the whole thing "embarrassing."

In search of a replacement, the Stalwarts wanted former president Ulysses S. Grant. Considered an American hero for leading the Union Army in the Civil War, Grant also allowed — willingly or not — lots of corruption. During his time in the White House, the spoils system flourished.

Nowhere did the spoils system show its true colors more than in New York City. New York was the home state of Senator

In this cartoon, Garfield is shown wrangling crooked politicians.

Roscoe Conkling, somebody who rose through the spoils system to become one of the most powerful men in the country. He had worked hard years earlier to help Ulysses Grant win the presidency, and Grant appointed Conkling one of the most prized positions. He put him in charge of the New York Customs House.

And Grant appointed Conkling's best friend, Chester Arthur, as head collector of the Customs House.

In this time before the government collected income tax, it leaned heavily on import fees. About 70 percent of all imports coming into America came into this New York building and required fees. The goods going through this one building were responsible for one-third of the money that supported the U.S. government.

Conkling could appoint whomever he pleased to any of the high-paying jobs at the Customs House. And he could demand in return their loyalty in money and votes for him and the Republican Party. He enjoyed this position, and used it to great advantage. Naturally, in 1880 he originally wanted Grant to get the Republican nomination.

A different group of Republicans, those known as the Half-Breeds, stood up to the Stalwarts and called for reform. These two groups battled it out during the 1880 convention in Chicago that, when all was said and done, chose Garfield as the nominee. And how Garfield dealt with the spoils system as president showed his backbone and determination for fairness.

★★★

Meanwhile in the South, troubles continued for former slaves who had been freed by President Lincoln's Emancipation Proclamation and by the 13th amendment in 1865. Fifteen years later, these free people faced violence when they attempted to vote in elections or to exercise other basic freedoms.

Garfield did not make many campaign speeches, but his most significant one took place in front of 50,000 people in New York. He spoke about the need to treat black Americans with the respect they deserved. Recalling the Civil War, he said no black man was a traitor and no Union solider was ever betrayed by a black man anywhere. He felt he needed to speak out about this. Many white

Young residents of a settlement near Savannah, Georgia, in the 1880s; at the time of Garfield's candidacy, many African Americans across the South were being denied freedoms promised to them by the 13th and 14th amendments, which banned slavery and required equal protection under the law for all Americans.

Americans, it seemed, had stopped caring about issues faced by black Americans now that the Civil War was finished and slavery was forbidden. But Garfield knew that although slavery was over, black people were anything but safe in the Southern states. Killings, beatings, and other violence continued against African Americans by angry Southerners still upset over losing slavery.

Former slave and anti-slavery leader Frederick Douglass spoke to a massive gathering in October 1880. He insisted to his largely black audience that Garfield "must be our next president" as he understood the difficulties of black American lives after the Civil War. Because of Garfield's own beginnings, he could understand and address issues of homelessness and poverty. "He has shown us how man in the humblest of circumstances can rise, win," Douglass said.

Garfield knew that Southern blacks would be threatened with violence when they sought to vote. Assuming he'd lose Southern states as a result, he realized he'd have to win New York. That's why he needed to be on the good side of Roscoe Conkling.

Frederick Douglass

Garfield accepted Arthur as his vice presidential candidate, but the two were not cut from the same cloth.

The party chose Conkling's friend Chester Arthur to be Garfield's running mate. Arthur had never held office. It was a move Garfield was not happy about but knew he needed to accept.

And that move worked. Conkling felt confident he would be able to keep his role at the Customs House. He threw his support behind Garfield, who won the November 1880 election by a very close margin.

Garfield was sworn into office March 4, 1881. The early days of his presidency were filled with interviewing people who sought jobs in the administration. They were seeking many positions that, in the past, would have gone to an incoming president's friends and supporters.

When Conkling visited the president, he expected to be told he would continue to run the Customs House. But Conkling received some bad news. Garfield decided against putting him in charge of the Customs House. The president explained that his choosing Chester Arthur as his running mate had been his gesture of gratitude to Conkling. The senator was furious, and Garfield expected as much. "I owe something to the dignity of my office," Garfield explained to a friend.

Public response to the decision seemed to agree with Garfield, but Conkling wasn't finished. Vice President Arthur, still more loyal to Conkling than the president, argued against Garfield's decision. Arthur even signed protest petitions against the president.

Then Conkling took a gamble he surely later regretted: He quit the U.S. Senate as a public protest against the president. He did so with the assumption that the New York Legislature — in charge of electing senators back then — would vote to bring him back. Thus, Conkling figured, he would have made his point by walking out on the president only to be voted back in by the New York Legislature.

Garfield basically scoffed at the move, calling it a weak attempt at drama. More and more people agreed. One congressman claimed it was a "great big baby boohooing because he can't have all the cake."

Conkling's plan backfired. He was never elected back into the Senate. His power was slipping dramatically. His only connection to power was in Chester Arthur, a man who in a few months, would be president.

A political cartoon from 1881 depicted the resignation of Roscoe Conkling and Thomas Collier Platt from the U.S. Senate.

Charles Guiteau posed this picture shortly before he

CHAPTER 4
GUITEAU'S CRIME

On May 18, 1881, Charles Guiteau believed God was speaking to him — and telling him to kill the president of the United States. That's what Guiteau would claim many months later. Guiteau insisted to his jailers, his jury, and anybody else who would listen in the meantime that he had heard the voice clearly tell him what to do. The voice said the new president needed to be out of the way for the Republican Party to succeed. This voice came to Guiteau not long after he received bad news. He was told that his hope of the new president giving him a job was not going to happen.

Imagine a mind already unable to sort out fantasy from reality. Imagine a life of constant high hopes met with constant failure. Now add to that a big dose of anger and embarrassment. What does it add up to? In Guiteau's head, it led not only to a voice telling him to kill the president, but convincing him it was a good idea for the country.

He also believed that, after the killing, he would be thanked by a grateful nation.

"(Garfield) has proved a traitor to the men that made him," Guiteau wrote in a letter to be read after the assassination. "This is not murder, it is a political necessity. This will make my Friend Arthur president and save the Republic. I expect president Arthur and Sen. Conkling will give the nation the finest administration it has ever had."

In his criminally crazed mind, he didn't have much room for the idea that he might get into some trouble for killing the president. He figured he'd be arrested and jailed for a while, sure. But he also planned on getting pardoned and thanked by would-be President Chester Arthur.

Once Guiteau was convinced to move ahead with the murder, he considered how and when to do it. He also spent lots of time thinking about all the fame and publicity it would bring. He even started to re-write an old book he had published during his unsuccessful days as a preacher. Once he was famous, he figured, the book would probably be in high demand. He had titled it, "The Truth: A Companion to the Bible."

Needing a weapon for his deed, Guiteau borrowed money and bought what at the time was a very expensive pistol. He picked that pistol not because it would deliver a better shot, but because it looked good. That was only proper, he thought, for something that was sure to become a national treasure.

Oddly, as Guiteau was planning his crime, he continued to write letters to President Garfield. He wrote to urge Garfield to give in to Roscoe Conkling's demands. The president never wrote back.

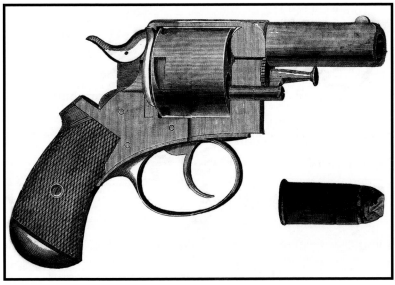
Engraving of Guiteau's English Bulldog Pistol, the gun used to kill President Garfield

Guiteau found himself with plenty of opportunities to kill Garfield before the day he pulled the trigger. He had made it a practice of following the First Couple to various events, once coming close to shooting the president during a church service. Guiteau knew he could find Garfield regularly at the Vermont Avenue Christian Church. That was where Garfield had attended since coming to Washington as a congressman. Before his presidency, Garfield had taught Sunday school there and pitched in to work when the church needed a bigger building. Armed with his gun, Guiteau attended a service and sat behind the president. The president was unprotected. Guiteau had his chance. For whatever reason, he chose not to shoot the president then. Instead he shouted at the preacher during the service.

Today it would be unthinkable for the president of the United States to stroll on his own down a street on his way to church or a restaurant. In 1881, however, the idea of a protecting the president's every move was seen as unnecessary. Even though a previous president, Abraham Lincoln, had been killed by an assassin, that crime was viewed largely as a shocking result of the Civil War. People didn't think such a thing would happen again, especially during times of relative peace.

After all, the American system of government allowed for the country to get rid of an unpopular or bad president peacefully — by voting him out. No need for bloodshed, storming a castle, or overthrowing someone who would otherwise cling to power for life. The United States — a little more than 100 years old at the time — had a system that put the head of the government up to vote every four years.

Guiteau, a tragic bug in that system, had read in the newspaper of the president's plan to travel to visit his wife at their New Jersey home on July 2. That morning, Guiteau woke early. After a walk in Lafayette Park, he went to the Baltimore and Potomac Railroad Station and waited.

In addition to his gun, he carried two letters with him. One was to William Tecumseh Sherman, chief of the army, and the other was addressed to the White House. In the letter to Sherman, Guiteau explained in a series of short sentences that he was going to jail for shooting the president and would like Sherman to order his troops to take over the jail. In the letter to the White House, he wrote with calm logic, explaining that he was doing what needed to be done. He called Garfield's death a "sad necessity," but one that was needed to save the Republican Party and save the country. He wrote with a chilling, matter-of-fact tone that Mrs. Garfield would be better off this way, rather than watching her husband die of natural causes. Since Garfield was a Christian, wrote this failed preacher, he'd be happier in heaven than on Earth.

Guiteau arrived at the train station around 8:30 a.m. Within an hour President Garfield and Secretary of State Blaine arrived. No bodyguards were present, of course, just an assistant carrying their bags.

The three walked several steps into a carpeted waiting room before Guiteau approached from behind the president. Standing just three feet away, Guiteau fired his first shot. It grazed Garfield's arm, and the president shouted, "My God, what is this?" As the president began to turn around, Guiteau fired a second shot that

No bodyguard was on hand to keep Guiteau away from the president.

pierced Garfield's back just above the waist. The president fell forward, the back of his gray summer suit darkening with blood as onlookers rushed to make sure Guiteau didn't escape.

Witnesses said the look on Guiteau's face went from serious while taking the first shot to terrified after taking the second. As the president fell, Guiteau made a run toward an exit door. One bystander blocked his way out, and as Guiteau ran for another door, a ticket agent grabbed him and held on, shouting, "This is the man." Police already at the station kept Guiteau from the hands of an angry crowd. Guiteau told the police, "I want to go to jail."

Garfield was in agonizing pain, and it wasn't going to get better. The first doctor to treat the president was Dr. Smith Townsend, the city's health officer. Garfield was not at death's door. His wounds seemed serious but not devastating. In fact, he would remain alive for several months, and he likely would have survived the shooting entirely were it not for poor medical care. The president's poor care began with Townsend inserting his fingers into Garfield's back wound to search for the bullet.

Neither Townsend nor the doctor who would take over Garfield's care were concerned about germs. The science of germs and infections was new, and Garfield's doctors from start to finish were not believers.

In an eerie coincidence, Robert Todd Lincoln, whose father had died from an assassin's bullet years earlier, was at the train station when Garfield was shot. Lincoln brought to the scene the same doctor who tended to Abraham Lincoln's shooting. That man was Dr. Willard Bliss.

Bliss, who had been a war surgeon during the Civil War, took over Garfield's care from that day forward. He began by moving the president from the station to the White House. While Guiteau alone committed the crime, Bliss would someday share blame for Garfield's death. The doctor allowed few others to treat Garfield and resisted any other medical opinions on his care.

Bliss certainly didn't bother giving any time to the idea that germs could cause problems. The doctor didn't understand the need for sterile tools and a clean wound. In this, he wasn't alone. Many, if not most, U.S. doctors at the time still rejected the idea of tiny germs causing big problems.

That discovery had come about in the mid-1860s by a Scottish surgeon named Joseph Lister. (He's the namesake of Listerine mouthwash, which famously "kills germs that cause bad breath.") He believed germs played a role in patients' getting worse during surgery, that germs in the air and elsewhere were making their way into the open wounds. Lister experimented in surgeries by spraying disinfectant over the patient and wound during the operations. Infections in these circumstances went way down. Over time, of course, this became accepted science.

But the world of medicine would not change soon enough for James Garfield. His doctor thought this was a silly idea, getting an infection from something you couldn't even see.

After the shooting, days passed and the president struggled to stay alive. In a rush to help, inventor Alexander Graham Bell offered his latest invention — a metal detector — to help locate the bullet in Garfield's back. Dr. Bliss was so sure of himself that he allowed only the president's right side to be examined. He

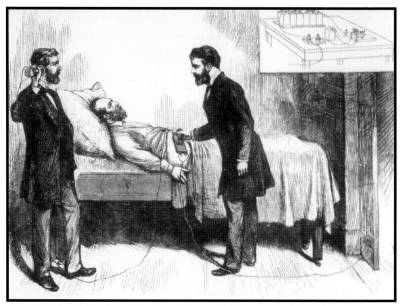

Alexander Graham Bell used a new invention of his to search for the bullet in Garfield's body, but he was advised to search in the wrong area.

was convinced that's where the bullet would be found. It was not there.

For weeks the public watched and waited, learning of the president's health updates through the newspapers. There were high hopes, then low ones. On September 6, Garfield was taken by a special train to his summer seaside cottage in New Jersey. There, it was hoped, the ocean breeze might help his condition. It didn't. On September 19, at 10:35 p.m., the president died.

An autopsy showed that the bullet was indeed lodged within the left side of Garfield's body. That was, of course, the opposite of what Bliss thought. There was a long, open path through the right side of Garfield's body. Bliss had assumed this was caused by the bullet. But the wound was determined to have been caused by fingers and instruments used in searching for the bullet.

Doctors also discovered that much of Garfield's body — his ears, the middle of his back, his shoulders, and his kidney area — were all poisoned with infections. He even had pneumonia in both of his lungs. Infection is what ultimately killed Garfield. The bullets started his problems, but they alone could not have killed him.

In her book on Garfield, biographer Candice Millard wrote: "It became immediately and painfully apparent that, far from preventing or even delaying the president's death, his doctors very likely caused it."

The coffin of President James Garfield, lying in state in the rotunda of the U.S. Capitol

A cartoon depicted Chester Arthur with a white elephant that resembled Roscoe Conkling, meaning Conkling had become unwanted and troublesome to the new president.

CHAPTER 5
THE AFTERMATH
OF THE ASSASSINATION

In the end, the death of President James Garfield likely helped accomplish something it may have taken him years to do. In response to the assassination, Congress soon passed a law that got rid of the spoils system.

President Garfield's shooting and eventual death had upset and angered citizens throughout the country. Rich or poor, they questioned how and why something like this could happen. What would motivate such a crime? As Garfield suffered and eventually died, people learned hard truths. Newspapers described the spoils system and how it worked like a big club that did favors for members only. Reports revealed how Charles Guiteau, expecting a nice job from Garfield, went mad when he didn't get it.

Like Garfield, the American people began insisting this system come to an end. They wanted government reform. They wanted politicians who would pledge to seek it as well. The big question

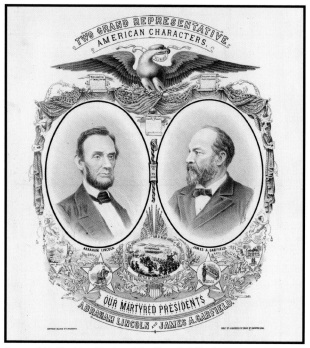

A memorial to President Lincoln and President Garfield, whose assassinations were the first in the country's history and came only 16 years apart

was how the new president, Chester Arthur, would deal with the system that made him so successful. That question was answered quickly. Starting with his first public speech as president, Arthur made clear his support for reform. Then in the 1882 elections, many in Congress who supported the old system were voted out of office.

One year into his presidency, Arthur signed into law The Pendleton Civil Service Act. This law completely changed the system. While government jobs were once given to men based on favors and friendship, the law required that they go to the people who were best for the jobs.

Perhaps nobody was more surprised by Arthur's decision than Roscoe Conkling. No longer in the U.S. Senate, Conkling had to be feeling pretty good now that his old friend was the new president. It was Conkling, after all, who was largely responsible for Arthur becoming vice

President Chester A. Arthur

president and, thus, assuming the presidency after Garfield died. Conkling was ready to have some favors returned.

In a move that would have seemed normal years before, Conkling began telling Chester Arthur what to do. For starters, he wanted Arthur to replace the man who had Conkling's old position of running the New York Customs House. Not that Conkling wanted the job. He wanted something else. He wanted to be appointed Secretary of State.

Conkling, however, got bad news. His old friend was no longer somebody he could push around. Arthur outranked him now and had far more power. Arthur was president of the United States. Arthur denied both of Conkling's requests. Conkling left Washington feeling angry and betrayed. He was so upset that he refused to accept Arthur's offer to place him on the U.S. Supreme Court.

Arthur's actions worked well for him. Those who doubted he would clean up the system were happy to be proven wrong. His popularity rose. His image improved. Still, he did not muster enough support to get re-elected. His own party chose a different candidate. When it came time to nominate a candidate in 1884, the Republicans chose James Blaine (who would lose the presidential election to Democrat Grover Cleveland). Arthur left the office far more popular a figure than when he entered it, and he died two years later at the age of 56.

In November 1881, less than two months after Garfield's death, the trial of Charles Guiteau began. It would stretch into the early days of January 1882. Guiteau's lawyers argued that he was innocent by reason of insanity. They said mental disorders prevented him from thinking straight and knowing right from wrong. The prosecutors, in response, said Guiteau knew full well what he was doing. They said that he knew it was wrong to shoot the president but did it anyway — and should pay the price.

Guiteau behaved horribly at the trial, often yelling and insulting his lawyers or interrupting people giving testimony. During the trial, three dozen medical experts took the stand to talk about insanity and mental illness. It was the jury's job to decide if Guiteau was guilty of knowingly killing the president or if insanity clouded his reasoning and guided his actions.

When it was his turn to testify, Guiteau spent nearly an entire week's time on the stand. He insisted he was instructed by God — the "Deity," in his words — to "remove" Garfield. Asked if he disliked the president, Guiteau said he considered him a "personal and political friend."

Guiteau at trial for the murder of President Garfield, 1881

"I simply executed what I considered the divine will for the good of the American people," he said. He also explained that if Americans knew better, they would not call Guiteau an assassin, but a patriot.

"I want it distinctly understood that I did not do that of my own personal volition, but on the inspiration of the Deity," he said. "I never would have shot the president on my own personal account."

To which the prosecutor asked, "Who bought the pistol? The Deity or you?"

But Guiteau stubbornly refused to take responsibility for killing Garfield, shifting all blame to the "Deity."

As the trial came to a close and both sides made their best case to the jury, Guiteau himself was allowed to address them. He decided to sing a song — "John Brown's Body" — and warned the jury that if they found him guilty "the nation would pay for it."

That didn't seem to bother the jury. It took less than one hour for them to meet and decide that Guiteau was guilty. The judge sentenced Guiteau to death by hanging. The assassin appealed the decision, even writing to President Arthur and asking for time to appeal to the U.S. Supreme Court. But his fate was sealed. Guiteau was executed at the District Jail in Washington, D.C., on June 30, 1882. Before he was hanged, he read a biblical passage and a poem of his own which ended with, "Glory Hallelujah! Glory Hallelujah! I am with the Lord!"

Not long after Garfield's death, the medical community embraced the work of Joseph Lister. He was the Scottish surgeon who believed germs played a role in patients' failure to recover from wounds or surgery. Many people realized the safer, cleaner procedures might have saved the president's life.

Lister went on to become one of the most admired men in medicine. He was honored by kings and queens. Doctors around the world began using antiseptics in surgery, which dramatically lowered the rate of deaths from infections. In 1902 the American ambassador to England praised Lister at a celebration honoring the doctor. According to the ambassador, Lister deserved to be thanked not only by doctors or by the United States, but "humanity itself."

The same medical community had harsh words for Dr. Bliss. He was accused of botching Garfield's care, particularly when it came to causing infections in the president's wound. Also, American surgeons blamed him for damaging the country's reputation for surgery.

Bliss, however, never admitted doing anything wrong. He

shocked Congress when he billed the government $25,000 for his work. (That would be about $500,000 today.) Congress instead offered $6,500, which Bliss angrily refused.

Garfield's goal of cleaning up the spoils system would see movement thanks to Chester Arthur's support of a new civil service law. Civil rights for black Americans, however, would not get much attention from Washington following Garfield's death.

Garfield knew that freed slaves in the South were anything but free. Even after slavery was outlawed and blacks could vote, they were routinely treated miserably in many Southern states, threatened and often killed if they attempted to vote.

Knowing firsthand that education was important to a good life, and that most blacks were illiterate, Garfield recommended a universal education system in which the U.S. government would fund education throughout the country. The idea never made it to Congress.

"Had he lived," wrote a scholar at the University of Virginia's Miller Center, he would have kept the issue "at the forefront of his administration."

Civil rights did not advance during Arthur's presidency. If anything, he went the opposite way by signing into law the Chinese Exclusion Act, which put a 10-year ban on Chinese immigrants, the first such law of its kind. (The concern was that too many Chinese were taking American jobs.)

In the Southern states, laws separating blacks from whites in schools, restaurants, transportation, theaters, and other public buildings continued through the end of the century. Violence against blacks became a way of life well into the 20th Century.

Garfield is memorialized with a statue in Cincinnati, Ohio, his home state.

Although James Garfield did not get the chance to be a great president, he did briefly bring about a shift in the American mood. Because of the kind of man he was, an entire nation — ripped apart by the Civil War mere years earlier — came together to hope for his recovery and to mourn his loss. As one biographer wrote, in the days after his death "his countrymen mourned not as northerners or southerners, but as Americans."

TIMELINE >>>>>>>>>>>>>>>>>>>>>>>>>>

Nov. 19, 1831: James Garfield is born in Ohio; his father dies when James is still an infant, leaving him to be raised in poor conditions by his mother

Sept. 8, 1841: Charles Guiteau is born in Illinois; after his mother dies when Guiteau is 7, he is raised by a violent father

1859: Guiteau enters the Oneida religious sect

1859: Garfield is elected to the Ohio state senate

Nov. 6, 1860: Abraham Lincoln is elected president

April 12, 1861: Southern forces fire on Fort Sumter in South Carolina, and the Civil War begins

August 1861: Garfield leaves his political office and is made a lieutenant colonel in the Union Army, soon promoted to colonel

January 1862: Garfield makes a heroic name for himself by leading a Union triumph at the Battle of Middle Creek and is soon promoted to brigadier general

November 1862: Garfield is elected to the U.S. House of Representatives

Jan. 1, 1863: President Lincoln issues an order freeing slaves in rebel states

Nov. 8, 1864: Lincoln is reelected as president

April 9, 1865: The South surrenders and the Civil War ends

April 15, 1865: President Abraham Lincoln is assassinated

Dec. 6, 1865: The 13th Amendment, abolishing slavery, is approved

1880: Guiteau begins his involvement in Republican Party politics, with hopes of winning favor with party leaders

July 8, 1880: Garfield, a U.S. senator, is chosen as Republican presidential nominee

Nov. 3, 1880: Garfield is elected president of the United States

March 4, 1881: James Garfield is sworn in as president of the United States

July 2, 1881: Guiteau, distraught over not getting an appointment, shoots Garfield in a Washington, D.C., train station

Sept. 19, 1881: Garfield dies after months of ineffective medical care

June 30, 1882: Guiteau, after a trial and verdict of guilty, is executed; he sings a religious song of his own creation on the gallows

GLOSSARY

antiseptic—a substance that kills germs and prevents infection

civil service—jobs working for the government

convention—the meeting during which a political party chooses its candidates for major offices

corruption—willingness to do things that are wrong or illegal to get money, favors, or power

customs—a government agency that collects taxes and gives permission for goods to enter or leave a country

disinfectant—a substance that stops or slows the growth of tiny, disease-carrying organisms

execution—to put a person to death as punishment for a crime

half-breed—an offensive term meaning the offspring of parents of different races; members of a moderate faction of the Republican Party in the years around 1880 were called Half-Breeds; they favored civil service reform

industrial— having to do with a type of business or manufacturing

nomination—choosing someone as a candidate for political office

spoils—valuable goods or services gained in return for a favor

stalwart—outstanding strength and vigor of body, mind, or spirit; members of a faction of the Republican Party in the years around 1880 called themselves Stalwarts; they opposed civil service reform

SOURCE NOTES

Page 14, line 22: Millard, Candice. *Destiny of the Republic: A Tale of Madness, Medicine and the Murder of a President*. New York: Doubleday, 2011, p.46.

Page 24, line 18: Ibid, p. 107.

Page 36, line 7: Ibid: p. 109.

Page 36, line 22: Ibid: p. 109.

Page 40, line 3: "Murder of a President." Narr. Michael Murphy. *American Experience*. PBS Television. 2 Feb. 2016.

Page 52, line 28: Hayes, H. G. and C. J. *A Complete History of the Life and Trial of Charles Guiteau, Assassin of President Garfield*. Philadelphia: Hubbard Bros. Publishers, 1882, p. 271.

Page 55, line 17: Ibid, p. 276.

Page: 57, line 6: *Destiny of the Republic: A Tale of Madness, Medicine and the Murder of a President*, p. 146.

SELECT BIBLIOGRAPHY

Hayes, H. G. and C. J. *A Complete History of the Life and Trial of Charles Guiteau, Assassin of President Garfield*. Philadelphia: Hubbard Bros. Publishers, 1882.

Millard, Candice. *Destiny of the Republic: A Tale of Madness, Medicine and the Murder of a President*. New York: Doubleday, 2011.

"Murder of a President." Narr. Michael Murphy. *American Experience*. PBS Television. 2 Feb. 2016.

Ridings Jr., William J. and Stuart B. McIver. *Rating the Presidents*. New York: Kensington Publishing Corp., 2000.

Rutkow, Ira. *James A. Garfield*. *The American President Series*. New York: Times Books, 2006.

ADDITIONAL RESOURCES

READ MORE

Barber, James. *Presidents*. New York: DK Publishing, 2017.

Kent, Deborah. *James A. Garfield: America's 20th President*. New York: Scholastic, 2004.

Langston-George, Rebecca. *The Booth Brothers: Drama, Fame, and the Death of President Lincoln*. North Mankato, Minn: Capstone Press, 2018.

Peterson, Amanda. *The U.S. Civil War: A Chronology of a Divided Nation*. North Mankato, Minn.: Capstone Press, 2015.

INTERNET SITES

Use FactHound to find Internet sites related to this book.

Visit www.facthound.com

Just type in 9780756557157 and go.

INDEX

ABOUT THE AUTHOR

JOE TOUGAS

worked for 17 years as a daily newspaper reporter and editor and is the author of several books for young readers. He lives in North Mankato, Minnesota, and his website is joetougas.com.

PHOTO CREDITS